MW01484290

Words of Wisdom

Mama U

SPEAKS ON BUSINESS AND LIFE

inspired and compiled by

Corliss A. Udoema

Copyright© 2022

Author	Corliss Udoema
Publisher	DBC Publishing, Gloucester, VA
ISBN	978-1948149204
Cover Art / Cover illustration:	2022© Cover: Dawn Gardner

2020©: All copyrights are reserved. The author supports copyright, which encourages diverse viewpoints, promotes free speech, and creates a vibrant and rich academic culture. Thank you for buying an authorized copy and for complying with international copyright laws. You are supporting the author to continue to publish.

No part of this book, including interior design, cover design, icons, or pictures, may not be reproduced, and/or transmitted in any form, by any means (recording, electronic, photocopying, or otherwise) without the prior written permission of the copyright owner.

Copyright Notice

Independent of the author's economic rights, and even after the transfer of the said rights, the author shall have the right to claim authorship of the work and to object to any distortion, modification of, and/or other derogatory action in relation to the said work that could be deemed prejudicial to the author's honor or reputation.

No part of this book or images – black and white, or other renditions of images, are to be posted to any social media, Internet, and/or other digital media or platforms without prior written permission of the copyright owner.

Any actions taken by the reader in response to the contents of this book shall be solely at the reader's discretion and personal risk.

Trademarks

All brand names, product names, logos, service marks, trademarks, or registered trademarks are trademarks of their respective owners.

TABLE OF CONTENTS

ACKNOWLEDGMENT

Many have helped me on my journey, and the names are too numerous to list here. Your names are written in my heart.

I was always a daddy's girl, and in all my life, I can never forget his love and the way he made me feel that I could do anything. Thank you to my daddy, James Carl 'Pediac' Pearson.

I want to acknowledge Rose McElrath-Slade, a strong, intelligent, and savvy entrepreneur. I will never forget my first steps after retirement. I had not thought of starting a business after retirement or even dreaming of becoming a national, award-winning, and successful business owner. However, Rose forced me out of the retiree comfort zone and gave me a unilateral directive, "You are going to start your business." I will never forget those first steps after my retirement (from the government). Love you my sister!

I would like to thank Sascha Mornell, whom I affectionally call my "Mentson" (Mentor-Son), which combines his role in my life as a mentor and son. I admire and respect your role as an inspirational leader, world changer, and amazing person that you are, Sascha. You co-founded three companies with a global presence. Your encouragement, wisdom, and unwavering truth are a blessing to me. Your advice is always 'spot on.' Thank you for always being there.

Rose and Sasha, I owe both of you a debt of gratitude. If folks listen to and follow your advice, they will not only become millionaires; they can become multi-millionaires!

FOREWARD

It's not what you know but what you can teach. It's not what you have but what can you share.

One of the things I quickly learned in my career is it is impossible for me to be in multiple places and give one-on-one time to individuals. This book is my attempt to share thoughts, ideas, and encouragement for those that desire to start, build, and grow a business – hopefully, debt free.

I will continue to commit to sharing what has worked and has not worked for me. I want to encourage others to take the first step and to keep on taking the follow-on steps. I want people to laugh, to be kind, and to have faith in their ability to make it.

Finally, I want people to grab their success and never forget to reach out and help someone else when they have the power to do so.

INTRODUCTION & PURPOSE

The sales of this book financially support those who have served our great country – our veterans. One hundred percent of the sales of this book are used to fund military service members, veteran-owned non-profits, and veteran-related business grants.

This book of personal stories, tidbits of wisdom, and business advice are a reminder that taking small steps, with a determination to consistently deliver excellence, does work. Remember – where you start does not dictate where you can go nor limit the goals you can accomplish.

Think about an old, southern lady who migrated from a small town in North Carolina that started a business with less than fifty dollars, conducted the crawl, walk, and run process (and in that order), that ended as a successful multi-million-dollar, debt-free business. This 'old lady' was disabled and disadvantaged (starting with very little in terms of education, money, youth, or mobility), but she proved herself a capable (and 'able') businesswoman in achieving national, state, and local recognition while maintaining a fierce commitment to giving back to the community.

Her wisdom can be yours! Read, enjoy, learn, and follow her hard-earned advice!

WINDOW VIEWS

How often do we engage in conversations that lead to debates and disagreements? Many years ago, I was having a discussion with a colleague. Our discussion eventually became a disagreement because neither of us could see the other's point of view.

We often find it impossible to agree with someone else's point of view because, quite frankly, we just don't see it, no matter how hard we try. In other words, we have to see it to believe it.

One day a thought came to me. It was clearly an inspiration from God. I thought about a view from my window. Let's say from my *living room* window. I stand and describe that view accurately from my perspective (viewpoint). However, someone looking out of my *dining room* window would have a totally different view (outlook).

The answer is simple and easy to remember. Your view and your viewpoint depend on where you are standing. Two can describe their views. Both are accurate, yet both are totally different because they are not looking from the same window.

The moral of the story:

Mama U

Before you disagree with someone's view...make sure you are looking out the same window!

Words of Wisdom

Mama U

The seed that we planted *yesterday* becomes the hope for **today** and the harvest for **tomorrow**!

Words of Wisdom

Mama U

Do this daily:

have an "in spite of"

determination to succeed.

Words of Wisdom

Mama U

I focus on what's *possible* — NOT what's impossible.

Words of Wisdom

Don’t see what I see?
Maybe we aren't
looking through the
same window!

Words of Wisdom

Reflections

Words of Wisdom

ROOFTOP LEADER

How do you see yourself as a leader? There are many types of leaders: effective, compassionate, servant, team builders, etc. However, I will guess you have never heard of a rooftop leader. You have not heard of it because I coined that phrase to describe my leadership goals. You see, that is truly the type of leader that I aspire to be.

Let me explain.

As a leader, it is my responsibility, or rather my challenge to effectively lead as a servant leader while building a team that works well together. Although I may not agree with all of my team members' views, I must see their viewpoints and consider and respect them.

To achieve this, however, I must climb to the rooftop to see the teams' views. As the rooftop leader – I am at the top.

I am positioned on the rooftop as a servant leader who is effective, compassionate, and a team builder. I am committed to leading in such a way that, although my team does not see what I see, they will trust my vision – because they trust me!

The moral to the story:

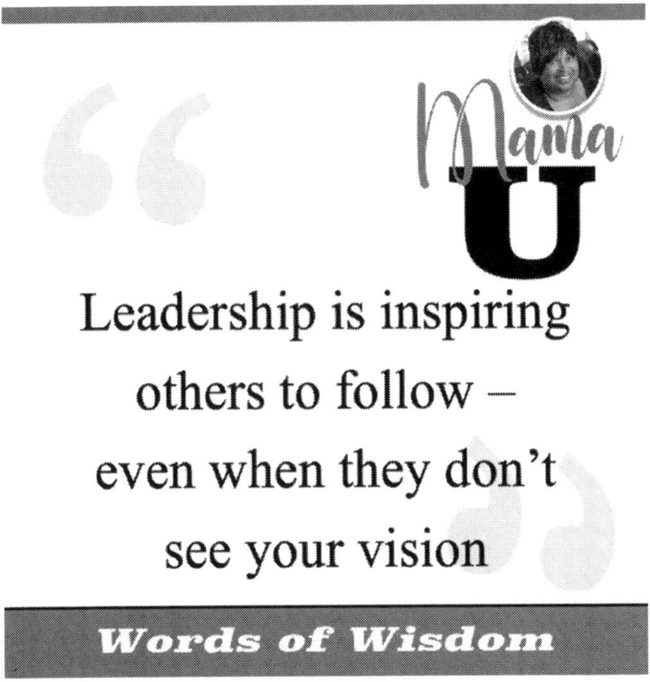
Mama
U
Leadership is inspiring others to follow – even when they don't see your vision
Words of Wisdom

Mama U

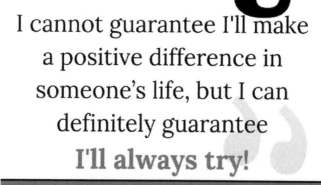

I cannot guarantee I'll make a positive difference in someone's life, but I can definitely guarantee **I'll always try!**

Words of Wisdom

Mama U

My life changed when I stopped *planting* seeds and started **sowing** seeds!

Words of Wisdom

Mama U

Teaching others what you've *read about* is quite different than teaching others **what you've lived**!

Words of Wisdom

You need to be **smart enough** to know what you don't know.

Words of Wisdom

Reflections

Words of Wisdom

STOP SELLING; IT DOESN'T WORK

Over the years, I have had many occasions to listen to the 'pitch,' the elevator speech, or the hook. It never ceases to amaze me how the most critical element is often omitted.

I was approached by one of my proteges about growing his customer base. He wanted to do a test run on his elevator speech. He began to talk about his company, background, and accomplishments. When he finished, he asked me how did he do?

Rather than answer him, I asked a question.

"If you had just painted your home, what would you do if a contractor called you and wanted to discuss his company's excellent painting services for an unbelievable price?

The contractor also shared information about his references, years in business, and the outstanding quality of his materials and workers. Would that motivate you to write a check?"

He said, "No."

I asked him, "Why not?"

He said he would not be interested because he did not need anything painted. Bingo.

I replied, "YES!"

When you have an opportunity to stand before a potential client, let us always remember it is not an opportunity to sell but to understand the client's needs and provide solutions to meet them. The goal is to be a service or product provider – consistently delivering excellence!

The moral of the story:

Mama
U
Stop focusing on what you can sell and focus on what you can provide!
Words of Wisdom

Mama U

Challenges may cause me to pause but **never to quit!**

Words of Wisdom

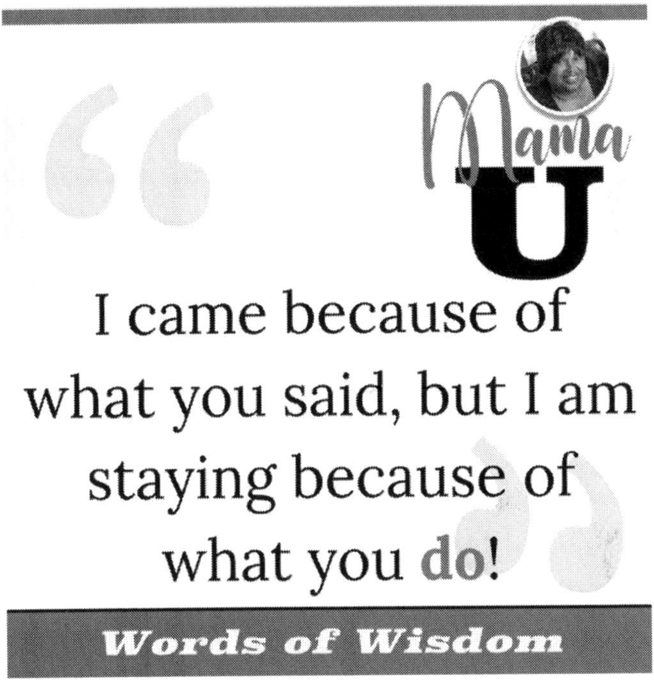
Mama
U
I came because of what you said, but I am staying because of what you do!
Words of Wisdom

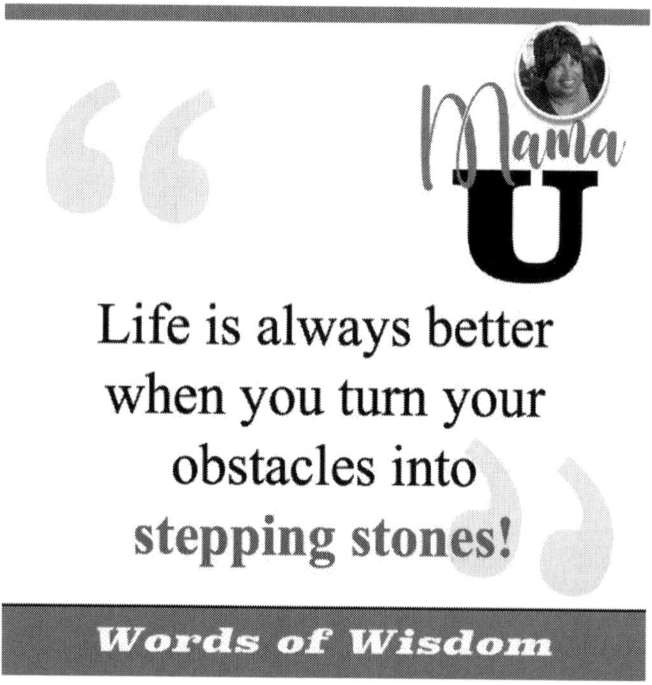
Mama
U
Life is always better when you turn your obstacles into stepping stones!
Words of Wisdom

Mama U

Recommendation for success: **don't ever give up!**

Words of Wisdom

Reflections

Words of Wisdom

CORN ON THE COB

Many times, we reject something because it is not all good. In life, we have to learn that everything offered does not have to be one hundred percent good or useful. I have shared this with others over the years as I would see them begin to reject things that were good and valuable because they were mixed with things of little or no value.

For those types of situations, I use what I call my corn on the cob theory. It simply means God has given all of us enough sense to know how to eat the corn off the cob and throw the cob away!

Often, we reject what could be very useful, the corn, because we solely focus on the cob, which is something not useful. Take it from me, never forget the value of the corn, and determine how you can benefit from it!

The moral of the story:

"God has given all of us enough sense to know we eat the corn off the cob and throw the cob away."

Words of Wisdom

Mama U

It's not what you have — **it's how you use it!**

Words of Wisdom

True faith is not only when you believe that God can – it is when you know that **God will!**

Words of Wisdom

Mama U

When you look at a big brick building, remember the importance of the mortar!

Words of Wisdom

Mama U

If you want to have successful *completions*, you need to know the value of a **'pit stop!'**

Words of Wisdom

Reflections

Words of Wisdom

KEEP DRIVING

This is my testimony about how you should never allow folks to convince you to give up.

Years ago, a friend and I were traveling from the District of Columbia to North Carolina in a snowstorm. After driving for several hours and traveling only about 100 miles, my friend suggested, "Let's pull over and spend the night?"

I said, "No," and kept driving.

It started snowing harder, and my friend urged me to stop. I kept driving.

My friend pleaded with me, sounding more and more panicky, “This is too dangerous, and we are going nowhere.”

I still kept driving.

Finally, my friend said, "Corliss, we've got to stop because this is really making me nervous."

I wanted to keep driving, but my friend was so upset I agreed and pulled over. We spent the night in the only motel available. It was definitely not our place of choice, but it was late at night, and we were not in an area that would likely have many options. However, we would soon learn that stopping at the motel would be more of a nightmare than driving in the snowstorm. As soon as we entered the room, we immediately discovered that the heat was not working! The room was freezing cold, so we had to sleep in our coats.

In the morning, we got back in the car to continue our journey, only to find that it was perfectly clear less than three miles down the road – not a single snowflake in sight! Always keep driving – even if family and friends tell you to stop! You may be only minutes away from coming out of your storm.

The moral of the story:

Mama U

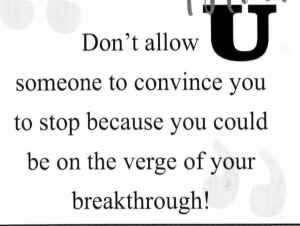

Don't allow someone to convince you to stop because you could be on the verge of your breakthrough!

Words of Wisdom

Mama U

I **choose** not to let my pain keep me from walking in my **purpose.**

Words of Wisdom

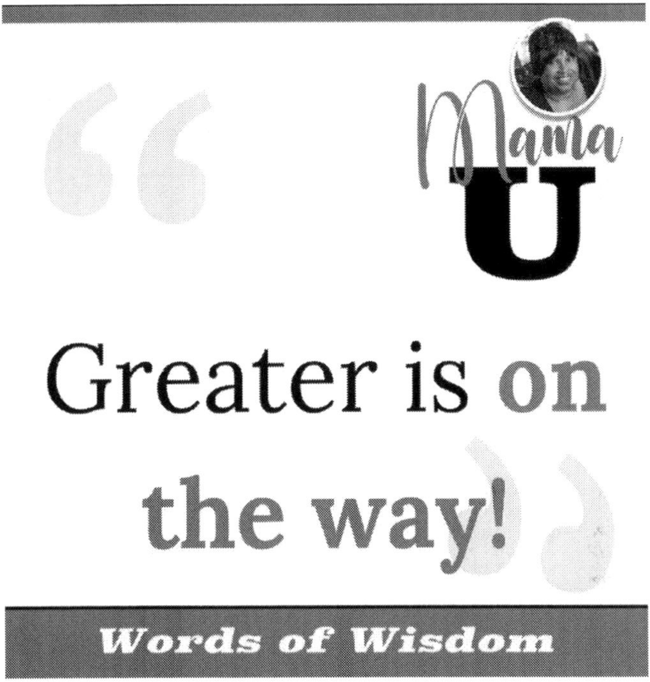
Mama
U
Greater is on the way!
Words of Wisdom

Mama U

Don't show up and deliver average.

Why not be great?

Words of Wisdom

Mama U

I'm forever grateful that my steps are ordered!

Words of Wisdom

Reflections

Words of Wisdom

HOLDING ON TO SOMETHING OF NO VALUE

Are you holding on to something that has no value?

It makes no sense to hold on to something that has no value because it will only take up valuable space in your life.

How do I know? Yes, you guessed it…because I did it!

Years ago, I was deeply hurt by someone. Even though the pain lessened over the years, I continued to hold on to the memory. It was like I was carrying a 50-pound bag of rocks.

One day I saw a vision of myself carrying around this 50-pound bag of rocks. The rocks, of course, represented the hurt and pain I experienced. I asked myself, "Why am I holding on to something that has no value?"

It was then I realized my determination to carry around that 50-pound bag of rocks had no benefit – it was of no value to me or anyone else!

That was the day that I let it go, the day that I stopped holding on to something of no value, the day that I stopped carrying around a 50-pound bag of rocks.

As you move forward in your life, I pray you will lighten your load and stop holding on to anything that has no value.

The moral of the story:

Mama U

Are you holding on to something that has no value? DON'T!

Words of Wisdom

Mama U

A small drop in the bucket … will eventually fill the bucket!!

Words of Wisdom

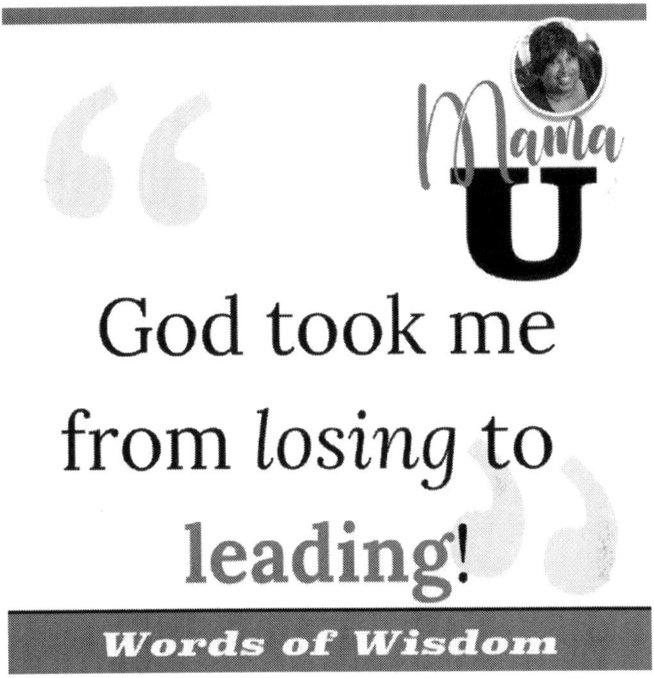
Mama U
God took me from losing to leading!
Words of Wisdom

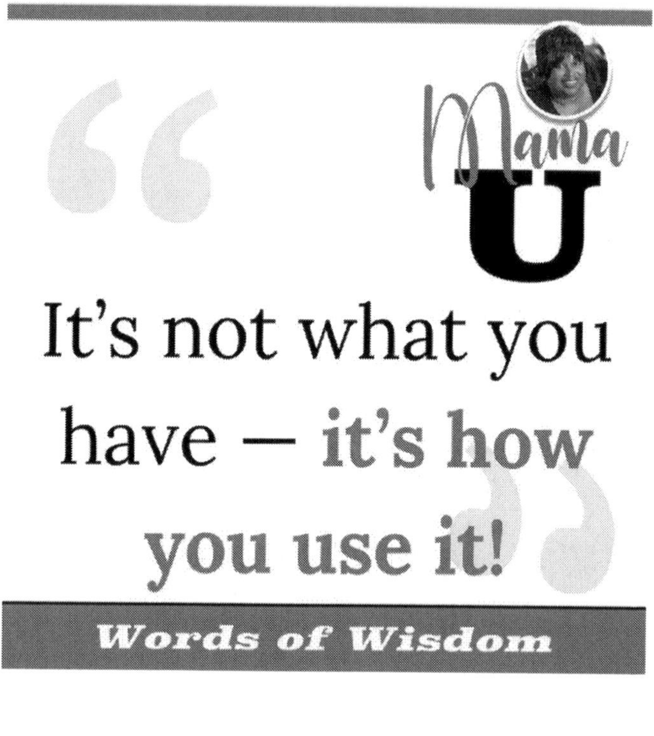
Mama
U
It's not what you have — it's how you use it!
Words of Wisdom

Mama U

Leave where you are *tolerated* and go where you are **celebrated**!

Words of Wisdom

Reflections

Words of Wisdom

OPEN THE BOX

Sometimes, simple situations can have a profound impact on your life. The pathway may not even always be complicated or complex. I reflected on my prayers when I asked God to send someone to help me.

You see, I had just moved from Virginia Beach to my new duty station in Japan. As was the customary practice, I had shipped essential items I would need until my household goods arrived. Everything was going according to plan until I received my shipment. The boxes arrived, and they filled my full-size van.

That was problem number one.

Problem number two – there was no one to help me.

The distance from where I parked my vehicle to my condo wasn't that far. At least, not far for someone that was young and fit. However, neither of those words described me.

So, now you understand my prayer request. I could not move the boxes on my own, so I prayed for God to send someone to help me, and let me tell you, pray I did! As days turned to weeks and weeks turned to months, I prayed even more, yet my prayers went unanswered.

On a very ordinary day at a very ordinary time, I pulled into the parking space at my condo and did a very unordinary thing…I fell apart. I started crying, letting God know that I felt forsaken. I reminded the Lord of his word…two are better than one because they have a better reward for their labor but woe to the one who is alone because if he falls, there is no one to pick him up. I cried out, “Lord, you took my husband, and if you don't help, I have no one.”

That day I cried so long and so hard that my stomach ached. I cried as I begged and pleaded, "Lord, please help me…I have no one but you."

If you have ever had that type of cry, you know that even when you stop crying, you need a moment to catch your breath as you move from uncontrollable sobbing to sniffles. It was now quiet. God spoke to me for the first time since I parked my vehicle. He spoke three words to me that changed my life.

"OPEN THE BOX!" He said.

I have been praying, begging, and pleading for over two months for help.

"OPEN THE BOX!" He said again.

I wiped my face, went upstairs to my condo, and returned to my van with two large suitcases on wheels. I followed God's words and opened a box, then another one, and another one. In less than an hour, I was in my condo with all of the contents from the now-empty boxes.

Do you know what God taught me with those three little words? He will give me the solution…all I have to do is tell Him the problem!

The moral of the story:

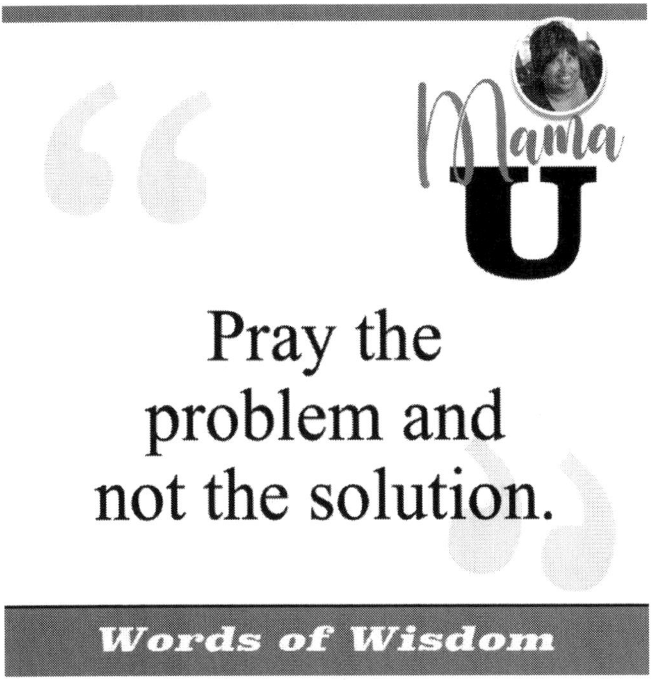

Mama
U
Pray the problem and not the solution.
Words of Wisdom

Mama U

When it's your season, nothing can stop you!

Words of Wisdom

Mama U

When thinking about what winners do, be sure to remember what they don't do...**QUIT!**

Words of Wisdom

Mama U

A candle doesn't lose its flame by lighting other candles.

Words of Wisdom

Mama U

I do a lot of things, but one thing I don't do: **Average!**

Words of Wisdom

Mama U

Reflections

Words of Wisdom

PICKING A TREE
OUT OF SEASON

I was sitting and taking a moment to reflect on my broken spirit. What did I not do? Where did I go wrong? How could my eyes have been open, yet I did not see what or who was in front of me? In Italian, they say, 'Che trova un amico, trova un tesoro,' which translates to "He who finds a friend, finds a treasure."

I remembered how we met and shared many late-night conversations on various topics. We began to call each other on a regular basis, have lunch, dinner, and sometimes even a movie. It was nice having a friend.

However, over time I began to see my friend was more different than we were alike. I was raised in a small rural community where we speak to everybody respectfully. We took time to greet each other because not doing so was rude and demonstrated your mama didn't raise you right.

I also noticed my new friend had very different criteria for who 'deserved' a hello. Her nonspeaking list kept getting longer, starting with maids and waitresses – basically, folks who provided services – and the homeless.

How could I have been so blind not to see our values were miles apart? I began to pray over how I was feeling and wondered how to end the friendship. I prayed for a peaceful, Christian, and non-offensive way to end the friendship.

I prayed for a 'Moses moment' – a moment that, even though I would be speaking the words and others would hear my voice, God would actually be speaking through me. The Lord opened my eyes to see what I had not seen before. It was time to speak, but before I did, I asked God how I did not see who was standing before me.

God said, "You picked a tree out of season. If you had waited for the tree to be in season, you would have known the tree by its fruit!"

Thank you, Lord. I shall never forget this lesson! Do you want to know how the relationship ended and if it was easy? I will answer the second part first. No, it was not easy.

The second part of my answer – the relationship ended with a few words. Not about the person that I once called a friend but rather words about myself. You see, I now had to face the fact that I never presented *myself* truthfully. All the times I didn't express my opinion that it was unacceptable not to speak to individuals based on their station in life was wrong. I confessed that.

So the relationship ended. Not because of what I said about the person but because of what I confessed about myself. In my transparency, the person that was once my friend saw the real me and decided I was no longer someone she wanted as a friend!

The moral of the story:

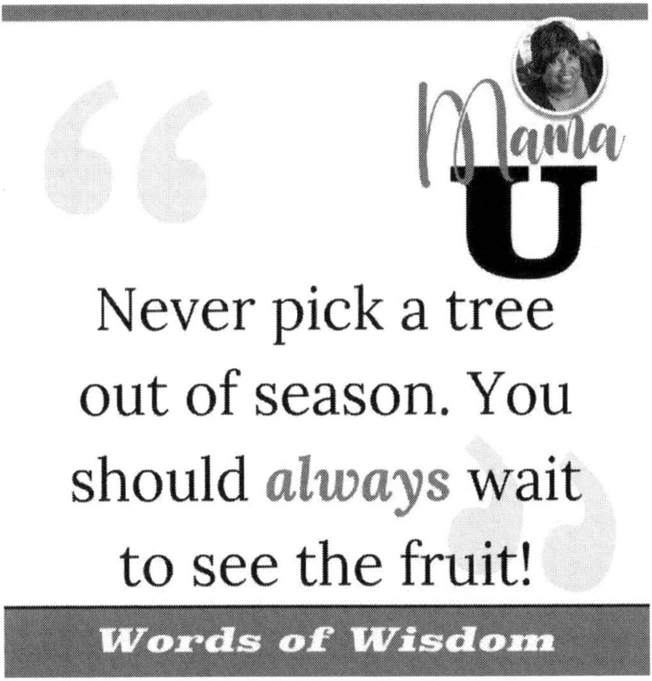

Mama
U
Never pick a tree out of season. You should *always* wait to see the fruit!
Words of Wisdom

Mama U

On your hardest days, have you ever looked back and noticed you see only one set of footprints?

Words of Wisdom

Mama U

"Don't miss a **blessing** by only judging the *outside*!"

Words of Wisdom

Mama U

It's time to shift your focus from what you've **lost** to what you have left.

Words of Wisdom

Reflections

Words of Wisdom

CRAWL, WALK, RUN, AND IN THAT ORDER

I started my own business after I retired from the federal government. Starting a business was something I had never considered. However, a very dear friend who is a dynamic businesswoman asked me to help her with a project because of my background in government contracting.

Of course, I said, "Yes."

When she asked me how much I would bill her, I replied, "No charge."

She told me, "*You* are starting a business, *you* will invoice me, and I will pay you."

If you knew my friend, you would understand her part of the conversation was one-way. The only thing I could do was start my business.

Start my own business? Hmm. I have been an entrepreneur since I was a child. I had worked as a senior-level contracting officer, and I had evaluated countless proposals. But, I had never written a proposal. I didn't believe I knew anything about being a government contractor on the 'other side of the table.' Was it time for me to be a 'beltway bandit' (euphemism for a federal government contractor)?

One thing I did know was my first step was to outline a plan of action. After supporting the military for 20-plus years, I knew trying to start without a plan was not an option. For some reason, 'baby steps' came to my mind. As I reflected on baby steps, I said to myself; first, the baby crawls, then they walk, and finally, they can run. Not only is it important to identify the three essential stages, but it is also equally important to ensure the steps are taken in the right order! The order is always crawl, walk, and then run!

The moral of the story:

Mama U

Crawl, walk, run, and in that order.

Words of Wisdom

Mama U

Excellence is never optional.

Words of Wisdom

Mama U

It's not your fault if you
get knocked down.
But it **is** your fault if you
don't get back up!

Words of Wisdom

Mama U

Make each day count. You will **never regret it!**

Words of Wisdom

Mama U

Today, right now, this minute … learn to let go of **what you can not change.**

Words of Wisdom

Reflections

Words of Wisdom

PROJECTS AND PRAYER

I was just leaving the airport in San Juan, Puerto Rico. I was about to embark on what *could* be a career-ending project. I was exhausted; however, it was not from the flight. I was mentally exhausted from a sea of negativity. Thinking over all the negative vibes and comments, I began to second guess myself...could I accomplish this task?

I remember their words, “How do you expect to accomplish the task if four prior three-member teams couldn't do it and you are trying to do it alone?” If the words weren't spoken, their skeptical looks said everything...you can't possibly do it.

If anyone has ever assigned you a near-impossible project, you certainly can understand my situation. You need someone who will give you a word of encouragement, even if they don't mean it.

It was apparent that the person who recommended me for the assignment obviously didn't think I could do it. I was sure they only recommended me to see me fall flat on my face. Why didn't I realize this sooner? Yet, in a conference room full of an upward chain of command, when asked about the assignment, I confidently said I could do it.

The Captain even asked me, "Corliss, if we have had four three-member teams attempt this project and fail, how do you believe you alone can accomplish it?"

I said, “Sir, I am not sure what they attempted to do or how they did it, but I am going on this assignment covered in prayer.”

The room was deadly silent. After I said the words, I looked up, and my immediate supervisor looked at me. I knew she would come to me as soon as we were alone. Her words to me were always, “No religion.”

As expected, my supervisor came by my desk immediately after the meeting and asked about my response to the Captain ('covered in prayer').

My response to her inquiry was, "I just honestly answered his question."

Well, now about that project. The first challenge was a follow-up meeting with the Captain. He asked for a one-on-one with me. Yikes! The good news was there would be no witnesses to a potential disaster; the bad news was no one would be able to step in and rescue me.

The meeting was more of a step-by-step outline of what to do to accomplish the project. After taking three pages of notes from the Captain, I requested permission to ask a question.

He said, "Yes."

I asked, "Sir, do you specifically want me to do these tasks as you have stated, or do you want me to execute the project?"

He looked at me, puzzled, and asked, "Isn't it the same thing?"

I said, "No, sir. It is not the same thing. If I execute the tasks you have given me, I will execute them exactly as you have directed me, with no changes. If you tell me to complete the project, I will execute *what* needs to be done to complete it successfully. I will stop and ask for your direction or assistance if I see an obstacle that prevents me from successful completion."

I was not expecting the response I received from him. He looked at me with a big smile and told me to forget his tasks and execute the project!

Do you want to know how this story ended? Three words - *project successfully completed*!

The moral of the story:

Mama
U
Believe that you can, then DO it!!!
Words of Wisdom

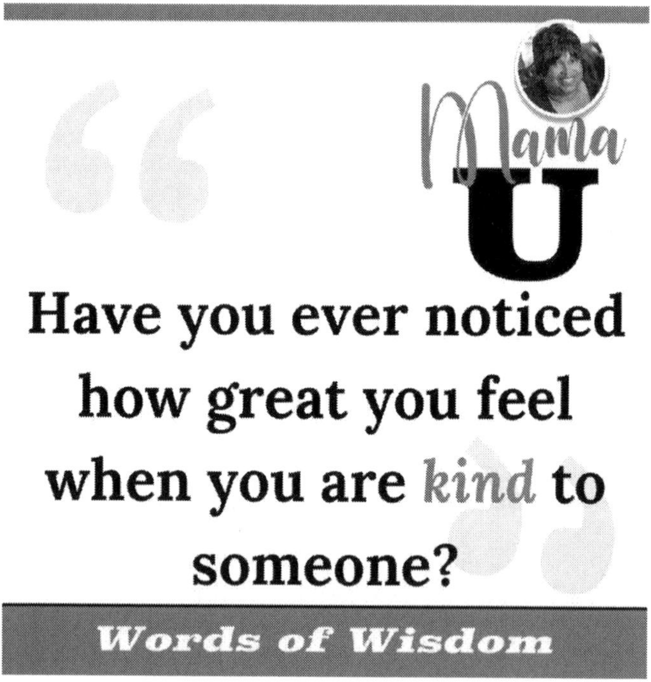
Mama U
Have you ever noticed how great you feel when you are kind to someone?
Words of Wisdom

Mama U

I don't measure my success by what I *have*, but by **the positive difference** I am able to make in the lives of others.

Words of Wisdom

Mama U

If you want wisdom, you must first **know the source!**

Words of Wisdom

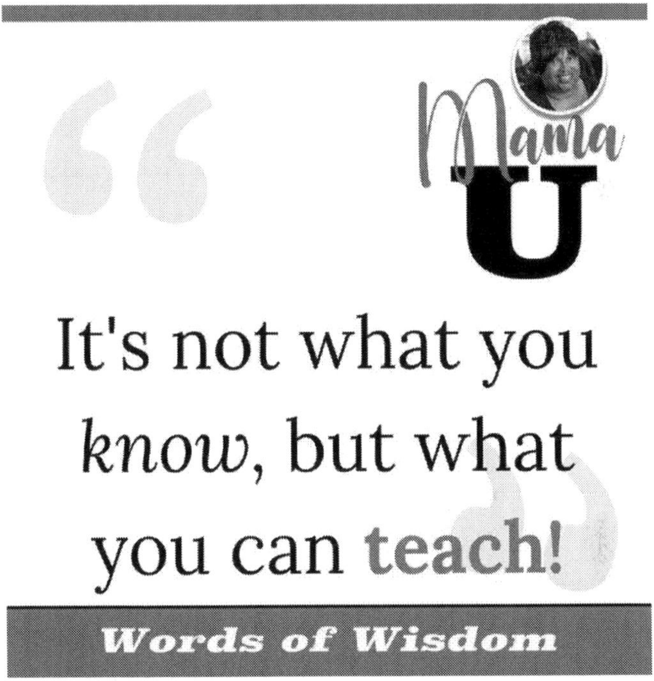
Mama
U
It's not what you *know*, but what you can **teach!**
Words of Wisdom

Mama U

Reflections

Words of Wisdom

A CLOSED DOOR IS NOT ALWAYS THE END

Thank God for closed doors.

In 2005, someone shared information about a leadership opportunity, and I decided to investigate the position. I had no idea how my life would change when I accepted the position as head of the Sanford Small Business Development Center – a small business incubator. Time passed quickly during the first year as I oversaw and finished renovations, leased office spaces to small business owners, hired staff, and developed training classes for small businesses. I set up a computer lab and developed computer classes for senior citizens. I loved what I was doing! I was helping veteran-owned and small businesses in the community get started, and I showed them how to grow.

After my first year, I beamed with joy and pride as I signed the new one-year renewal of my employment contract in Jan of 2006. All of my hopes and dreams were short-lived. A few weeks later, I found myself sitting behind a closed door in the director's office. The invitation to the meeting was unusual because a meeting topic was not shared with me. I never gave it much thought. I *should* have!

When I entered the room and was asked to close the door…something inside told me it was not good. The director shared that the project I was working on had run out of funding, effective January, the previous month in which I had signed that new one-year employment contract! I had a fully enforceable and legally binding contract. But God said, "*Forget your legal right, thank them for the opportunity, and gratefully walk away from that closed door.*"

So, I did what God told me to do.

Next came the miracle.

The same day the door closed, God led me to my first government contract opportunity. My new six-month contract paid me double my previous annual salary. The six-month relationship with that client lasted over ten years.

I thank God for that closed door! Don't believe closed doors are always the end. It could be the miracle start of a new opportunity.

The moral of the story:

Mama U

A closed door is
not always the end.
It could be a
new beginning!

Words of Wisdom

Mama U

The true test is believing what we **can not see!**

Words of Wisdom

Mama U

When you are a champion, not only will you roar – you will soar!

Words of Wisdom

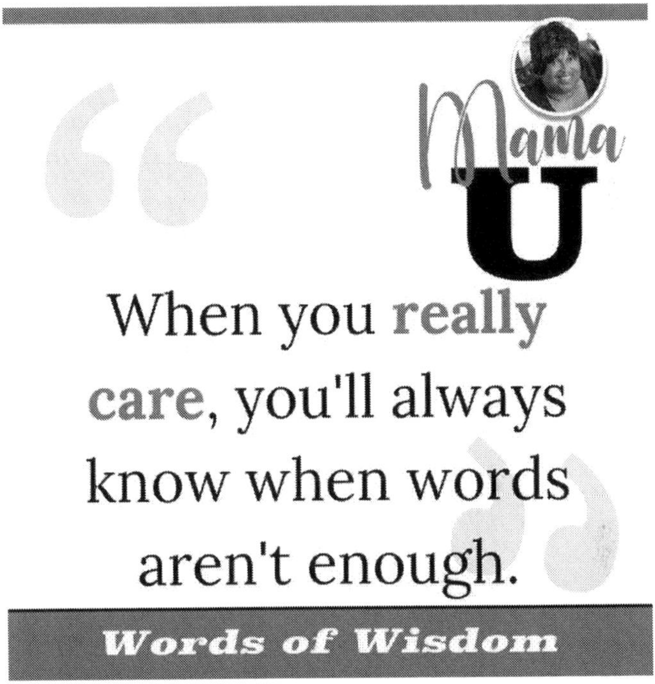
Mama
U
When you really care, you'll always know when words aren't enough.
Words of Wisdom

You *can* lead where you haven't been ... but you **can't** lead where you're not willing to go.

Words of Wisdom

Reflections

Words of Wisdom

Believe In What You Don't See

I started seeing small changes at first, and now and then, a new face or two on the floor where I worked. I had been working there for about a year. I knew everyone on our floor and the floor below where the senior management team was located.

No big deal at first, but as time passed, the number of new faces increased. In fact, they increased to the point I asked one of the government employees, "Who were the new folks?"

I was told they were new government employees. One or two…no issue.

By the time I had noticed at least eight or more, I thought I would get a few answers – if nothing else, at least to satisfy my curiosity. I shared my thoughts on all the new government employees with one of my coworkers. To my surprise, I was criticized for speaking 'negatively.' What on earth made that coworker respond in such a manner? I just walked away, feeling like I had spoken out of turn, determined to keep my mouth shut about the matter.

That was the spring of the year, and life went on as usual, but something inside me told me to keep a watchful eye. After a very nice and quiet summer, I again began to notice several new government faces.

I decided to ask about the new government employees. Again, I was told the new faces were 'new federal employees.' Nothing more, nothing less, with no explanation.

I again mentioned my concerns to one of my coworkers. You guessed it…my comments were not received well. In fact, the next day, I was told I had spoken negatively about our employment (again).

The coworker who criticized me, a pastor, told me I was speaking against God's blessing for our jobs. She even said in her prayer the night before, "God had told her to tell me, 'cease and desist.' Don't say another word about our jobs being in jeopardy."

I could not understand why God let me see what no one else was seeing. Nor could I understand why God told me to 'warn them of what was happening.' God's message to me was different than his message to my coworker!

So, after this last negative encounter, I left my desk and left the room for a one-on-one talk with the Lord.

"Lord, I am only doing what you told me, yet I am receiving a very negative reaction from my coworkers."

I shall never forget the response I received when I prayed about my coworker's reaction. The Lord said, "I told you to warn them; I never told you to remind them."

That is what we call a '*mike drop moment*!'

Time continued to pass, and now all the new government employees were on board. However, there was still no notice given to us about our jobs. In fact, our company had even hired a few more employees. Life was great. Business was good.

I did not see any evidence of our company losing the contract and losing our jobs. However, I decided to continue my preparations because of what I observed over the past several months.

I had already applied for a home loan, got approved, and moved into my house earlier in the year. The only thing remaining was to purchase a vehicle on the first of the year. I had money in savings – just in case.

The entire staff was in a great mood as the year-end holiday season started. When the company announced the big Christmas dinner, all eyes were on me. It seemed everyone knew about my 'doom and gloom' negative comments.

The news of the Christmas party planned by the company generated even more 'side eye' stares. The stares translated to 'I told you so! Our company is not going anywhere!'

The Christmas dinner was planned and scheduled by the company. Everyone had a great time. The food was delicious, and we all received awards and gifts. It was a fun event, but occasionally I would receive a few glances and comments, "I told you that you were wrong."

Although everything seemed to be in order, I still had doubts, no matter what my coworkers said. What could I do? Nothing, because God had already told me that He did not tell me to 'remind' them!

The holidays were over, and the first meeting in January was our monthly staff meeting. Everyone was still in a joyful mood, fresh from the holiday gift gifting, days off, and the amazing company Christmas party…until they heard the words, "We have lost the contract. Effective this month, we will be terminating two employees per month until everyone is gone."

Pandemonium…tears, profanity, and frantic phone calls to headhunters while the manager was still trying to control the meeting, to no avail. That was one time I did not have to be concerned about my coworkers giving me the look or comments. They were in shock and busy trying to find new employment!

I absolutely know – and I hope you will believe this – even if you don't see it. When God speaks…listen. By the way, because I was the last one to leave, I was the one who turned the lights out!

The Moral of the Story:

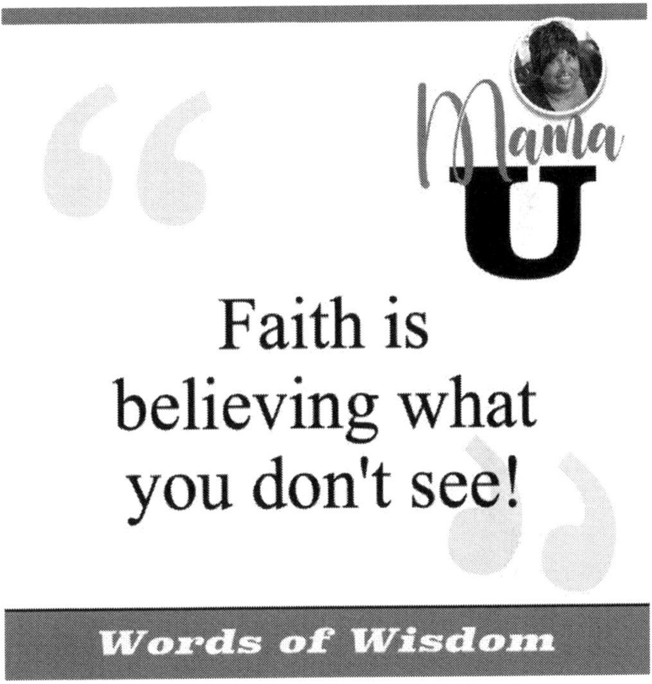

Mama
U
Faith is believing what you don't see!
Words of Wisdom

Mama U

The winning combination: spend, share and save!

Words of Wisdom

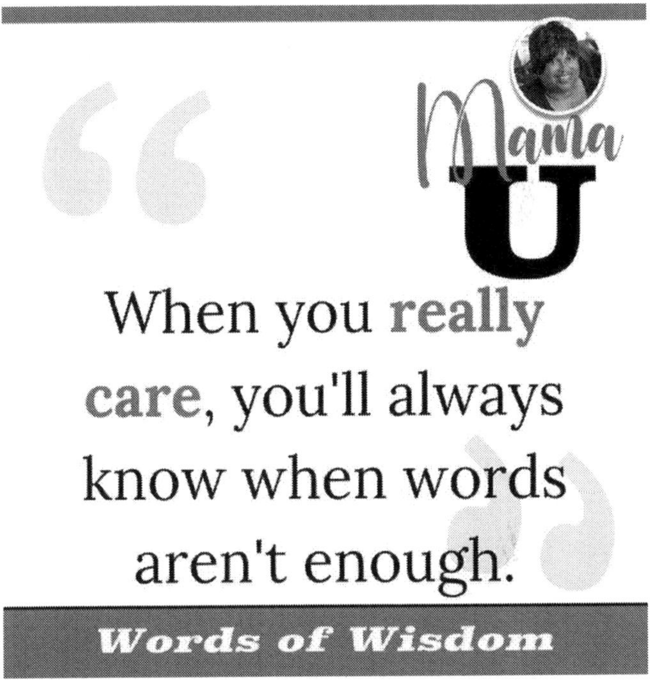
Mama
U
When you really care, you'll always know when words aren't enough.
Words of Wisdom

Mama U

When you're committed to success, you never have to *get* ready — **because you *stay* ready!**

Words of Wisdom

Mama U

You need to be **smart enough** to know what you don't know.

Words of Wisdom

Mama U

Reflections

Words of Wisdom

BONUS QUOTES

Mama U

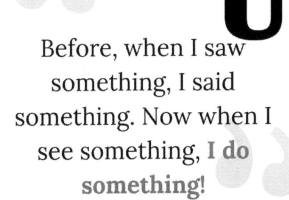

Before, when I saw something, I said something. Now when I see something, **I do something!**

Words of Wisdom

Mama U

Don't let *anyone* cause you to **lose your focus!**

Words of Wisdom

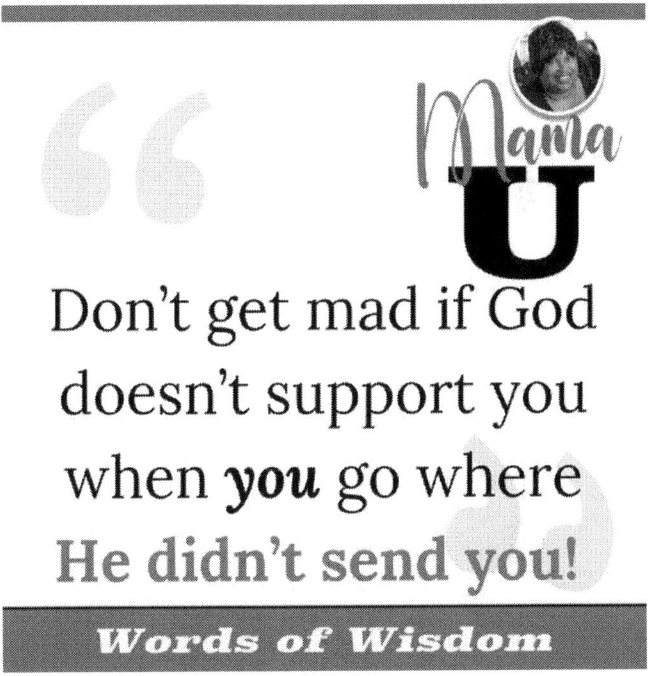
Mama
U
Don't get mad if God doesn't support you when **you** go where He didn't send you!
Words of Wisdom

Mama U

Are you determined to win? Then surround yourself with **champions**!

Words of Wisdom

About the Author: Corliss A. Udoema

Corliss A. Udoema is a preacher, evangelist, missionary, workshop facilitator, entrepreneur, and writer. Most of all, she loves the Lord and prays continuously for opportunities to lift the name of Jesus. Since early childhood, she has used her gifts of exhortation and administration to reach out to those in need. God has blessed Udoema to travel to fifty-nine countries and twelve islands, where she ministered, encouraged, and told the good news of Jesus.

She is a lifelong community worker and was recognized for her contributions to assist and improve the quality of life and fostering spiritual growth for those in need. She volunteered at Johnston Lee-Harnett Community Action, where she taught budgeting and financial literacy classes.

She is an internationally-accomplished, motivational speaker, and workshop facilitator. Over the 35 years, Udoema has developed and facilitated federal women's workshops, budget workshops, and religious retreats. She has served as a keynote speaker and workshop facilitator for government, non-profit, and faith-based organizations, including the General State Baptist Convention of North Carolina, Wyeth, and the North Carolina Continuing Education for Community Colleges

Convention.

Udoema received two Congressional awards for her work in small business development, was nominated by a US Congresswoman, and entered into the Congressional Record for her business and community service accomplishments. For the past five years (2017-2022), Udoema has received awards from the Washington Business Journal for charitable contributions and volunteer hours. Her company was ranked in the top three donors for five years. Her company was also ranked as one of the fastest-growing companies by INC-5000 for five consecutive years. Udoema was awarded the Small Business Person of the Year for the Commonwealth of Virginia (2017) and the third runner-up for the National Small Business Person of the Year (2017).

She is President of Agape Love in Action, Inc. (ALIA), a 501(c)(3) non-profit organization that reaches out to spread God's message of love by helping those in need. Udoema is involved with ALIA philanthropic efforts, including 'Hope in a Bag,' which provides support and services to homeless-shelter residents in locations throughout the United States, and Wisdom Meets Technology which provides computer literacy training and computers to senior citizens. In 2022, Udoema's non-profit, ALIA, founded a food bank that has donated thousands of pounds of food to those in need.

She was educated in the New Bern, NC, public schools and attended the University of Maryland. She carried on the work of an evangelist and a missionary her entire life and, in October 2002, accepted the call into the ministry. On July 13, 2003, Udoema preached her initial sermon at her home church in New Bern, NC, Mount Calvary Missionary Baptist Church, where her former pastor, Dr. C. D. Bell, presided.

Udoema retired from the Federal Government, where she spent almost 33 years in executive positions in the contracting, grants, and procurement arena. Since 2006, she has served as CEO and President of her international staffing and consulting company, Contract Solutions, Inc.

SUPPORTED CHARITIES

Agape Love in Action (ALIA), Inc.

ALIA's mission is to help those in need. Motivated by faith, ALIA serves alongside the poor and oppressed as a demonstration of God's unconditional love for all people. ALIA supports several outreach initiatives, including Hope in a Bag, Wisdom Meets Technology, Business Battle Buddy (financial support and coaching to veterans), and Reach 2 Feed. In addition, ALIA sponsors community outreach and development programs that bring together local service providers and the people in the community who require assistance. ALIA endeavors to address individuals' physical, emotional, mental, social, and economic wholeness, impacting families and changes in communities. ALIA collaborates with faith-based, corporate, academic, philanthropic, government, and community organizations to meet basic human needs of recipients by providing tools to enhance their lives.

For more information: http://agapeloveinaction.com/

About the Book

Corliss Udoema is the author of the book, *A Guiding Light: Poems and Reflections* (in which 100% of the sales support several non-profit charities). Udoema's life and business experience have inspired her to share what she calls her Words of Wisdom (WOW), which are easy to understand, thought-provoking, and simple to implement. *Words of Wisdom: 'Mama U' Speaks on Business and Life* is a refreshing, pocket-sized book of wisdom, enlightenment, and stories of insight – earned and learned – over several decades.

She shares her collection of wisdom in solid and down-to-earth nuggets of insightful quotes meant to challenge, encourage, educate, and incentivize. She offers her business and life wisdom to a broader audience to provide weekly advice to those who strive to be ethical, better, wiser, and stronger in their personal and business worlds.

The stories and quotes of wisdom are based on personal experiences and lessons learned that can be broadly applied to any situation in life for a more practical, positive, and enlightening resolution. The author listened to God and wrote the words as they came to her after experiencing personal, business, and emotional challenges. This book shows the author's heart and love for the Lord. Her deep and personal relationship inspired each story and quote of wisdom with the Holy Spirit.

Made in the USA
Middletown, DE
28 October 2022

13674719R00073